Super Singing Activities

A-Z ACTIVITIES TO MAKE SINGING FUN

Animal and Insect   Bird in the Leafy Treetops   Build a Prophet
Build a Snowman   Christmas Tree Sing with Me
City of Enoch Singing Meter   Fill Noah's Ark Pick-a-Song
Follow the Signs   Go Fishing!   Keyword Connection
Melody's Family Tree   Name that Tune   Pick-a-Card
Sunny Sunday Sounds   Temple Flowers: "Bee" a Singer
Super Singer Awards

Introducing the Author and Illustrator, Creators of the

Primary Partners series, *Young Women Fun-tastic!* series, *Gospel Fun Activities, Super Singing Activities, File Folder Family Home Evenings,* and *Home-spun Fun Family Home Evenings* series, found in books and CD-ROMs

MARY H. ROSS, Author

Mary Ross is an energetic mother, and has been a Primary teacher and Achievement Days leader. She loves to help children and young women have a good time while they learn. She has studied acting, modeling, and voice. Her varied interests include writing, creating activities and children's parties, and cooking. Mary and her husband, Paul, live with their daughter, Jennifer, in Sandy, Utah.

JENNETTE GUYMON-KING, Illustrator

Jennette Guymon-King has studied graphic arts and illustration at Utah Valley State College and the University of Utah. She served a mission to Japan. Jennette enjoys sports, reading, cooking, art, gardening, and freelance illustrating. Jennette and her husband, Clayton, live in Riverton, Utah. They are the proud parents of their daughter Kayla Mae, and sons Levi and Carson.

Copyright © by Mary H. Ross and Jennette Guymon-King
All Rights Reserved

Covenant Communications, Inc.
American Fork, Utah

Printed in China
First Printing: October 2002

Super Singing Activities
ISBN # 1-59156-060-8

COPYRIGHT NOTICE: Patterns in this book are for use by individual Primaries and individual families only. Copying patterns for any other use is prohibited.

ACKNOWLEDGMENTS: Thanks to Inspire Graphics (www.inspiregraphics.com) for the use of Lettering Delights computer fonts.

Introduction

Super Singing Activities: with Ready-to-Use Visuals

There is never a dull moment in Primary singing time and family home evening with these *Super Singing Activities*. Children will look forward to these singing time activities that encourage them to sing in a variety of ways. Use them each week along with the *Primary Partners Singing Fun!* book and CD-ROM to match the sharing time theme for the current year.

With these ready-to-use visuals you will save time and money, as the visuals are already colored for you. The pages are perforated, ready to tear out and use. Simply cut them out and you're on your way to making singing time fun. We suggest that you mount most of the visuals on cardstock paper and laminate for durability. Tear out the instruction pages and cut out each set of instructions to attach with visuals.

These singing activities were taken from the 1999-2002 sharing time *Primary Partners Singing Fun* books.

This book of visuals is also available to print in color and black and white from CD-ROM (shown right). This is especially helpful if you want to print more of the Super Singing Awards (pages 147-167) in color*.

SUPPLIES NEEDED FOR SUPER SINGING ACTIVITIES:
- scissors and cardstock or poster paper (to mount visuals) .... all activities
- clear Contact paper (to laminate visuals) .... all activities
- poster paper and sticky-back Velcro to mount visuals .... most activities
- file folders (to store activities) .... all activities
- artists spray adhesive (best & quickest), glue, or rubber cement . all activities
- poster and string .... page 37 *City of Enoch*
- tongue depressors (wooden sticks) .... page 55 *Follow the Signs* and page 117 *Stop and Go*
- fishing pole, string, magnet, and paper clips .... page 77 *Go Fishing*
- bottle ...... page 77 *Keyword Connection* and page 87 *Name That Tune*
- paper fastener (metal brad) and poster... page 117 *Sunny Sunny Sounds*
- *extra copies of awards .... page 147-167 *Super Singer Awards*

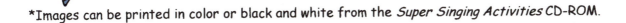

*Images can be printed in color or black and white from the *Super Singing Activities* CD-ROM.

To Prepare the Visuals to Be Used Again and Again:

The purpose of this book is to provide you with easy-to-use visuals. With the following tools and methods, you can produce visuals that can be used again and again. For durability, these visuals should be mounted on a heavier backing and then laminated. You will find that mounting the visuals on cardstock or poster paper increases the durability, and keeps the visuals rigid for easier posting on the board, walls, or poster for display purposes.

TOOLS: *You'll Need:* Artist's spray adhesive (best and quickest), glue, or rubber cement, cardstock or poster paper, scissors.

TO MOUNT VISUALS ON CARDSTOCK OR POSTER PAPER:

1. *Mounting Two-Part Visuals:* Tape them together on the back before mounting.
2. *Mounting Visuals:* Before cutting out the visual, spray the entire back of the visual using the artist's spray adhesive (best results), or evenly spread the glue or rubber cement over the entire visual and stick visual to your choice of rigid backing (cardstock or poster paper). Glues will require drying time before laminating or cutting out, but spray adhesive is ready immediately. Once the visual is stuck to the backing, you are now ready for cutting or laminating.
3. *Laminating Your Visuals:* Laminating increases the durability of your visuals and allows you to use the visuals over and over without tearing.
4. *Laminate Posters:* Consider laminating several large posters front and back to create a smooth surface. Then when you post the visuals, the tape won't tear or mar the poster paper.
5. *Laminating with a Machine:* Laminating done with a machine is the most durable, but it is not necessary. Clear Contact paper also creates a laminate surface. If you are machine laminating your visuals, cut them out first and then laminate. Once the visuals are laminated, cut the laminate 1/8th of an inch or more from the edge of the visual to keep the edges from separating from the lamination.
6. *Laminating with Clear Contact Paper:* If you are laminating your visuals using clear Contact paper, glue them to the backing first and then laminate. Cut the Contact paper the size needed to cover the visual. Separate the backing on one end of the Contact paper only a few inches. Position the Contact paper over the visual and as you slowly remove the backing, press the Contact paper on the visual to avoid any bubbles or creases. Repeat on the back of the visual and then cut out.

STORING YOUR VISUALS:

1. *Manila Folders:* Store visuals in a manila folder so that they will remain flat and away from the sun to prevent bending and the colors from fading.
2. *Larger Folders:* If you have larger visuals that will bend if placed in a manila folder, make a large folder using poster paper. Fold the poster in half and tape the left and right sides, leaving the top open.

Table of Contents
Super Singing Activities

1. Animal and Insect: Do as I'm Doing 1-8
2. Bird in the Leafy Treetops 1, 9-24
3. Build a Prophet—Pick-a-Song 25-32
4. Build a Snowman 25, 33-36
5. Christmas Tree Sing with Me 37-48
6. City of Enoch Singing Meter 37, 49-54
7. Fill Noah's Ark—Pick-a-Song 55-66
8. Follow the Signs 55, 67-76
9. Go Fishing! 77-82
10. Keyword Connection 77, 83-86
11. Melody's Family Tree 87-96
12. Name that Tune 87, 97-100
13. Pick-a-Card 101-110
14. Singing Simon 101, 111-116
15. Stop and Go! 117-122
16. Sunny Sunday Sounds 117, 123-134
17. Temple Flowers: "Bee" a Singer 135-146
18. Super Singer Awards 147-168

Activity #1: Animal And Insect Do as I'm Doing

Use this activity to help children get rid of wiggles prior to a sharing time presentation, prayer, or singing time. Children copy the motions of animals or insects as they sing, e.g., waving their arms like the butterfly flapping its wings.

TO MAKE:
1. Mount visuals (pages 3-8) on cardstock paper, laminate and cut out.
2. Place them in a container to draw from.

TO USE:
1. Sing the song "Do As I'm Doing," page 276 in *Children's Songbook* using motions found on the animal and insect circles.
2. To determine motion, have children draw a circle from a container, show the card and tell the others the motion.
3. Do the motion, e.g., "peck like a woodpecker," as you sing the song.

Activity #2: Bird in The Leafy Treetops

Use this activity to help children choose songs and sing in a different way by choosing a hidden song bird.

TO MAKE:
1. Mount visuals (pages 9-24) on cardstock paper, laminate, and cut out.
2. Write the names of songs children are familiar with or the ones you are practicing on the backs of leaves.
3. On the back of the five song birds, write one of the following on each: Sing standing up, sing with arms folded, sing with eyes closed, sing turned around, only boys sing, and only girls sing.
4. Hide the five birds behind the leaves by taping the bird to the tree and covering it with a leaf.
5. Place the tree on a poster or chalk board and tape the leaves around the tree, with the song birds hiding behind the leaves.

TO USE: Ask children to come up and choose a leaf. Sing the song on the back of the leaf chosen. If a child finds a song bird behind the leaf, ask children to sing the way the song bird suggests, e.g., eyes closed (see #3 above).

All images can be printed in color or black and white, using the *Super Singing Activities* CD-ROM.

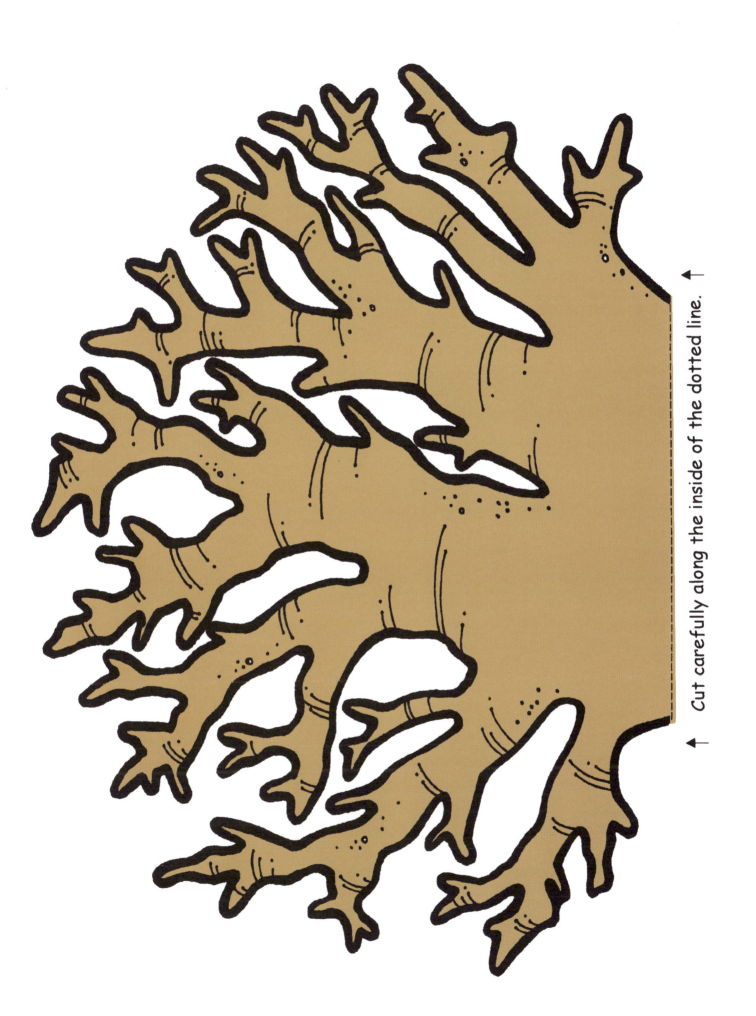

Super Singing Activities

Activity #3: Build a Prophet – Pick-a-Song

Use this activity to help children choose songs to sing by selecting and placing prophet pieces on a poster to "build" an ancient prophet.

TO MAKE:
1. Mount visuals (pages 26-32) on cardstock paper, laminate, and cut out.
2. Tape the visuals on a poster to show children and introduce the activity. Then take pieces from poster and place in a container or to the left of the poster on the board (mixed up).

TO USE:
1. Have children draw pieces from a container (without tape on the back), or taped on the board randomly.
2. As children place images on the board to build a prophet, have them choose a song to sing. Or have selected songs and page numbers on the back of each piece for children to choose which song they will sing.

Activity #4: Build a Snowman

Use this to help children choose a song. This is a fun winter time activity and keeps them interested in singing as they build the snowman.

TO MAKE:
Mount visuals (pages 33-36) on cardstock paper, laminate, and cut out.

TO USE:
Arrange the visuals randomly along the side of a poster or chalkboard, or put the pieces in a bag to draw from. When a piece is chosen, the child or leader can read the song and the child can tape the piece to the poster or board to build the snowman. Children can choose the pieces in any order, e.g., they can choose a nose before there is a face to put it on. Have them position it about where it will end up (or move the face if the head comes last, etc).

All images can be printed in color or black and white, using the *Super Singing Activities* CD-ROM.

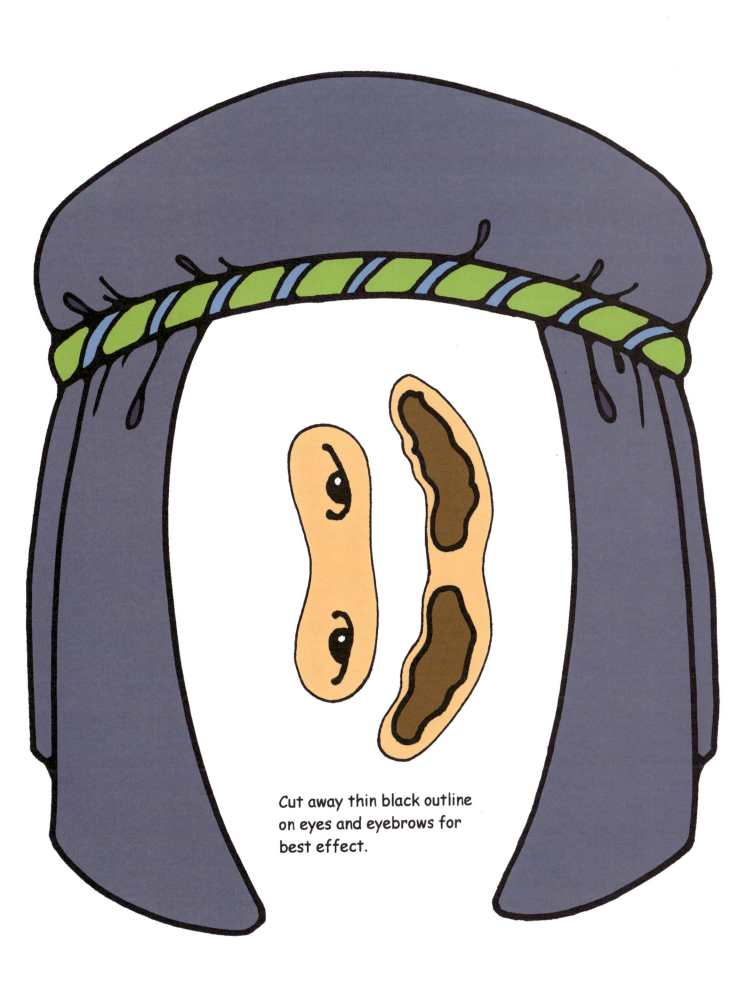

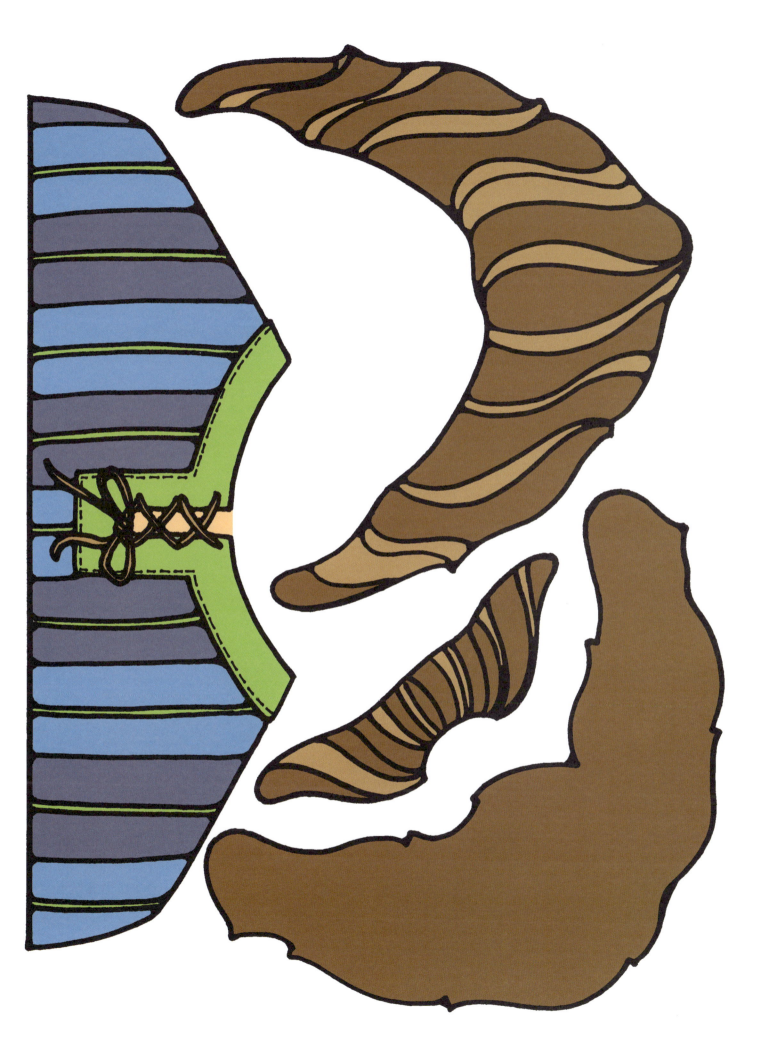

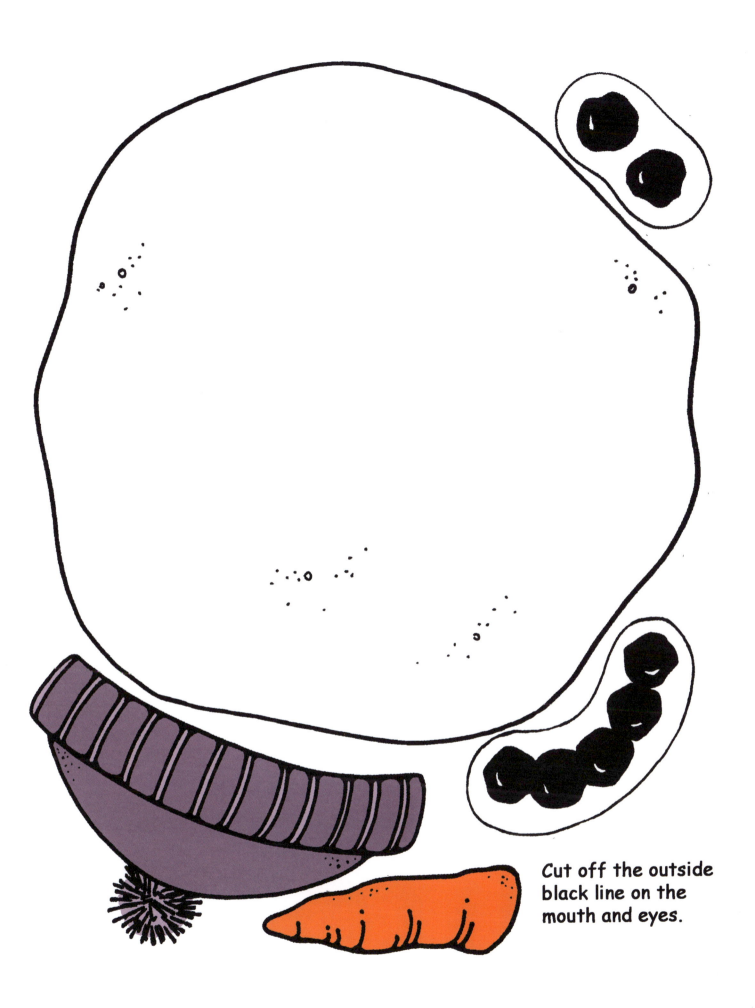

Cut off the outside black line on the mouth and eyes.

Super Singing Activities

Activity #5: Christmas Tree Sing With Me

Use this activity to help children sing Christmas songs found in the *Hymns* or *Children's Songbook*. The following are in the *Children's Songbook*: "Away in a Manger" (p. 42), "Christmas Bells" (p. 54), "Have a Very Merry Christmas!" (p. 51), "He Sent His Son" (p. 34), "Little Jesus" (p. 39), "Mary's Lullaby" (p. 44), "Oh, Hush Thee, My Baby" (p. 48), "Once within a Lowly Stable" (p. 41), "Picture a Christmas" (p. 50), "Samuel Tells of the Baby Jesus" (p. 36), "Sleep, Little Jesus" (p. 47), "Stars Were Gleaming" (p. 37), "The Nativity Song," (p. 52), "The Shepherd's Carol" (p. 40), "There Was Starlight on the Hillside" (p. 40), "When Joseph Went to Bethlehem" (p. 38), and "Who Is the Child" (p. 46).

TO MAKE:
1. Cut out tree parts A-C (pages 38-44) and mount to a large poster and laminate the entire poster.
2. Mount the ornaments (pages 44-48) on cardstock paper, laminate, and cut out.
3. Write and tape a song title and page number on the back of each ornament.

TO USE: Select from options #1 or #2.
Option #1: Have ornaments taped or attached with Velcro to the tree for children to choose ornaments, singing the song on the back. If using Velcro, use the sticky-back Velcro to place velcro on tree poster and ornament.
Option #2: Have children choose ornaments from a container or from visuals taped to the board. Sing the song on the back, placing the ornament on the tree.

Activity #6: City of Enoch Singing Meter

Use this activity to help children improve the quality of their singing, e.g., louder, softer, faster, slower.

TO MAKE:
1. Mount visuals (pages 49-54) on cardstock paper, laminate and cut out.
2. Mount the visuals on a poster with tape or the city of Enoch with string, (shown left) to pull up and down. To mount string, pierce a hole below "heaven" and above the "earth." Feed the string through the back and tie in the front. Attach the city of Enoch over the knot tie. Pull up and down from the back to raise or lower the city of Enoch.

TO USE:
1. Tell children about the prophet Enoch and his city of righteous people who were lifted up into heaven (Moses 6-7; Genesis 5:24, and in the *Old Testament Stories* p. 22).
2. Have a child or leader pull the city of Enoch up and down on a string or move up and down (mounted with tape) as children sing.

If the image moves up to heaven, they are singing well, or down to earth, they know they need to improve.

All images can be printed in color or black and white, using the *Super Singing Activities* CD-ROM.

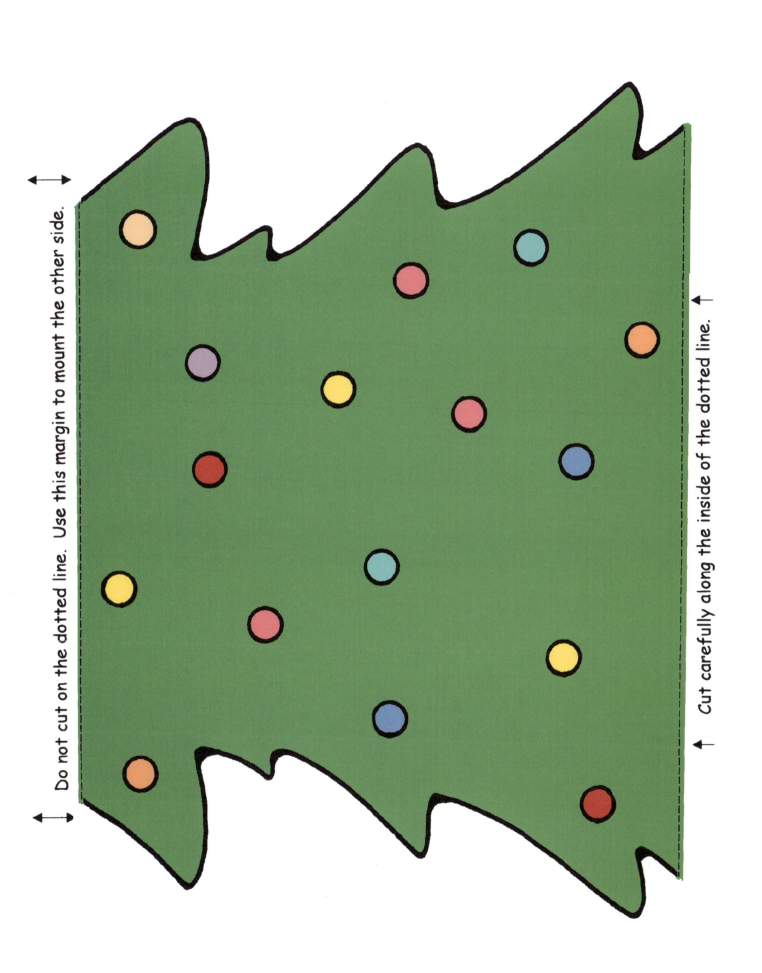

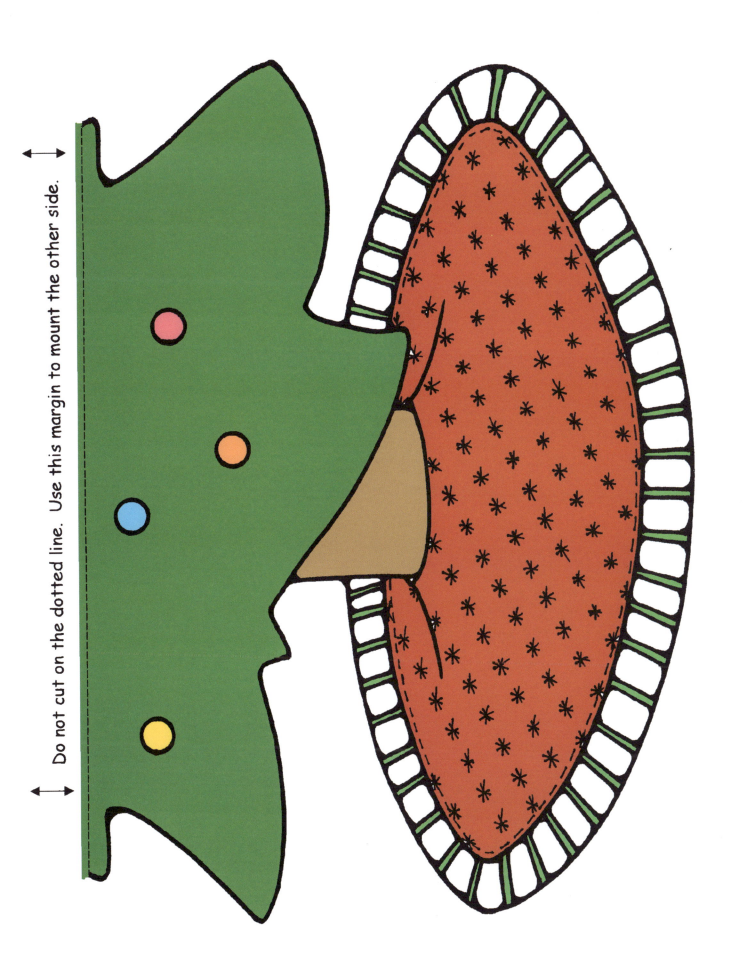

Super Singing Activities

Activity #7: Fill Noah's Ark—Pick-a-Song

Use this activity to help children choose songs to sing by selecting and placing Noah's family and animals in the ark.

TO MAKE:

1. Mount ark pieces, Noah's family and animals (pages 57-66) separately on cardstock paper, laminate and cut out. Cut the ark on the dotted lines so that Noah's family and the animals will fit into pockets once the ark is mounted on a poster.

2. Tape the ark pieces on a large poster so that the images placed in the slots will slide in easily.

Note: Mount on the poster paper, leaving a pocket, so that the hippo, elephant, and Noah can be inserted in the top of the ark.

TO USE:

Have children take turns drawing Noah's family and the animal pieces out of a bag or container and placing them in the labeled pockets.

Option #1: Song titles and page numbers can be written on the back of each image to indicate songs to sing.

Option #2: Images can be blank on the back. When a child draws a blank image they can name their favorite Primary song to sing.

Activity #8: Follow the Signs

Use this activity to help children choose songs and sing in different ways.

TO MAKE:

Mount visuals (pages 67-76) on cardstock paper, laminate, and cut out. *Optional:* Mount on sticks.

TO USE:

Option #1:

While the children are singing, the leader or a selected child holds up the desired sign one sign at a time to cue children to sing faster, slower, softer, louder, or to hum the song.

Option #2:

A leader can line up five children in front, holding the signs. The leader or another child can walk behind the child holding the sign and touch them on the head to show how the song should be sung.

All images can be printed in color or black and white, using the Super Singing Activities CD-ROM.

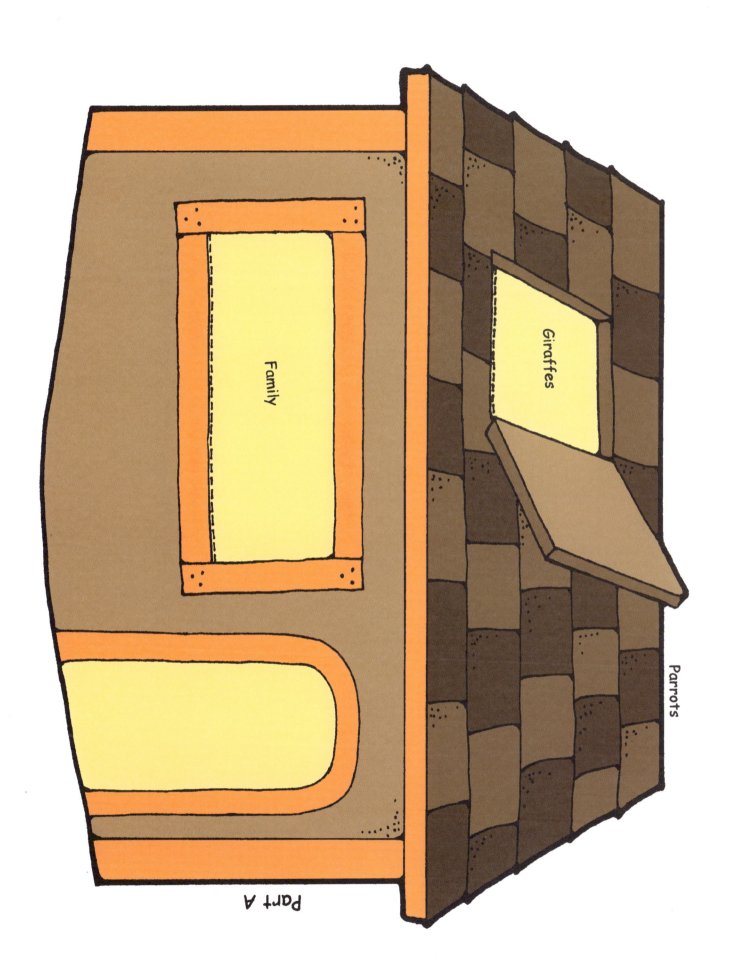

Activity #9: Go Fishing!

Use this to help children choose a practice song or other favorite song. Give children the opportunity to fish for a song by placing a song on the back of each fish.

TO MAKE:

1. Mount fish (pages 79-82) on cardstock paper, laminate, and cut out.
2. On the back of each fish, write the title and page number of a song the children know or a song you are currently practicing.
3. Make a pole by tying a string to a dowel or stick with a magnet at the end of a string.
3. At the mouth of each fish, attach a paper clip to be picked up by the magnet on the pole.

TO USE:

When you are ready for a song, tell children, "Let's go fishing for a song to sing." Children can read the fish or hand it to the leader to read the song.

Activity #10: Keyword Connection

Use this to help children choose a Primary song or hymn to sing that matches the keyword.

TO MAKE:

Cut out the *Keyword Connection* label and key words (pages 83-86). Mount the label on a wide-mouth bottle or container. Place key word wordstrips inside.

TO USE:

Choose children one at a time to draw a keyword from the container and read it aloud. The child then tries to think of a song that relates to that keyword. Tell children that the keywords can be a word in the song or the title. Or they can look for the key words in the *Children's Songbook* Index or Titles and First Lines. *Examples:* If the keyword "Families" is chosen, the child might choose "Families Can Be Together Forever," or "Family Night." The keyword does not have to be in the title. If the child wants to sing "I see my mother kneeling with our family each day," look in the Titles and First Lines Index. The words begin the song "Love Is Spoken Here" (page 190).

Child	Kindness
Commandments	Thankful
Family	Heavenly Father
Forgiveness	Light
Holy Ghost	Prayer
Jesus Christ	Spring
Love	Tithing
Missionary	Priesthood
Pioneer	Scriptures
Prophet	Happiness
Rain	Articles of Faith
Sacrament	Book of Mormon
Temple	Joseph Smith
Testimony	Example

Super Singing Activities

Activity #11: Melody's Family Tree

Use this activity to help children choose songs to sing by selecting and placing a family member on this Melody's family tree. Talk to children about the importance of families being together forever and finding the names and information of family members who have passed on. This way they can have their temple work done to seal families together forever, linking their loved ones who are on their family tree.

TO MAKE:
1. Cut out the tree (pages 89-96). Mount the tree on a poster and laminate the entire poster.
2. Mount the family member figures (pages 93-94) on cardstock paper, laminate and cut out.

TO USE:
1. Have children draw Melody's family member figures from a container.
2. As children choose and place images where they belong on the family tree, have children choose a song to sing. Or tape selected songs and page numbers on the back of each piece.

Option: Have ways to sing songs on the back of family member figures. Examples: a cappella (without music), girls only, boys only, standing up, sitting down, with chin up, with arms folded, standing facing backwards.

Activity #12: Name That Tune

Use this activity to help children listen carefully to recognize favorite Primary songs and hymns.

TO MAKE:
1. Cut out the *Name That Tune* label (page 97) and mount it on a wide-neck bottle or container.
2. Cut out the Primary song wordstrips (page 99) and enclose in the bottle or container. *Note:* Select songs they are familiar with.

TO USE:
1. Have children take turns drawing a tune (song title) from the bottle or box and handing the paper to the pianist.
2. The child drawing the song keeps it a secret. That child tells the pianist to play one note or two.
3. The pianist plays the first and second note and the children try to guess the song.
4. The child who guesses the song correctly comes up to draw the next song. If no one guesses the song after three tries, the child who drew the song chooses another child to come up and draw a song.

All images can be printed in color or black and white, using the *Super Singing Activities* CD-ROM.

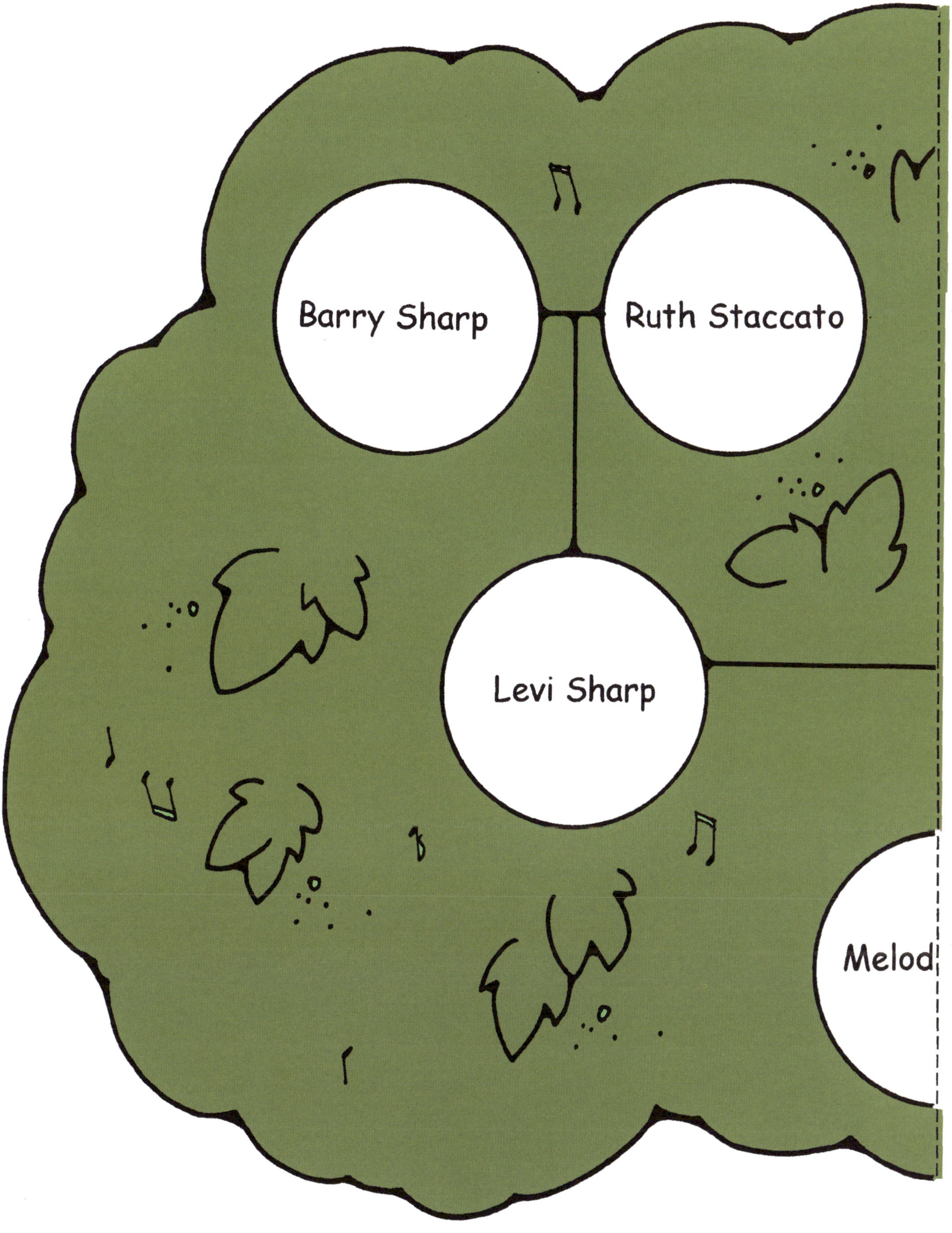

Barry Sharp

Ruth Staccato

Levi Sharp

Melod

Cut carefully along the inside of the dotted line.

Fester Tempo

Rose Vibrato

Mary Tempo

y Sharp

Do not cut on the dotted line. Use this margin to mount the other side.

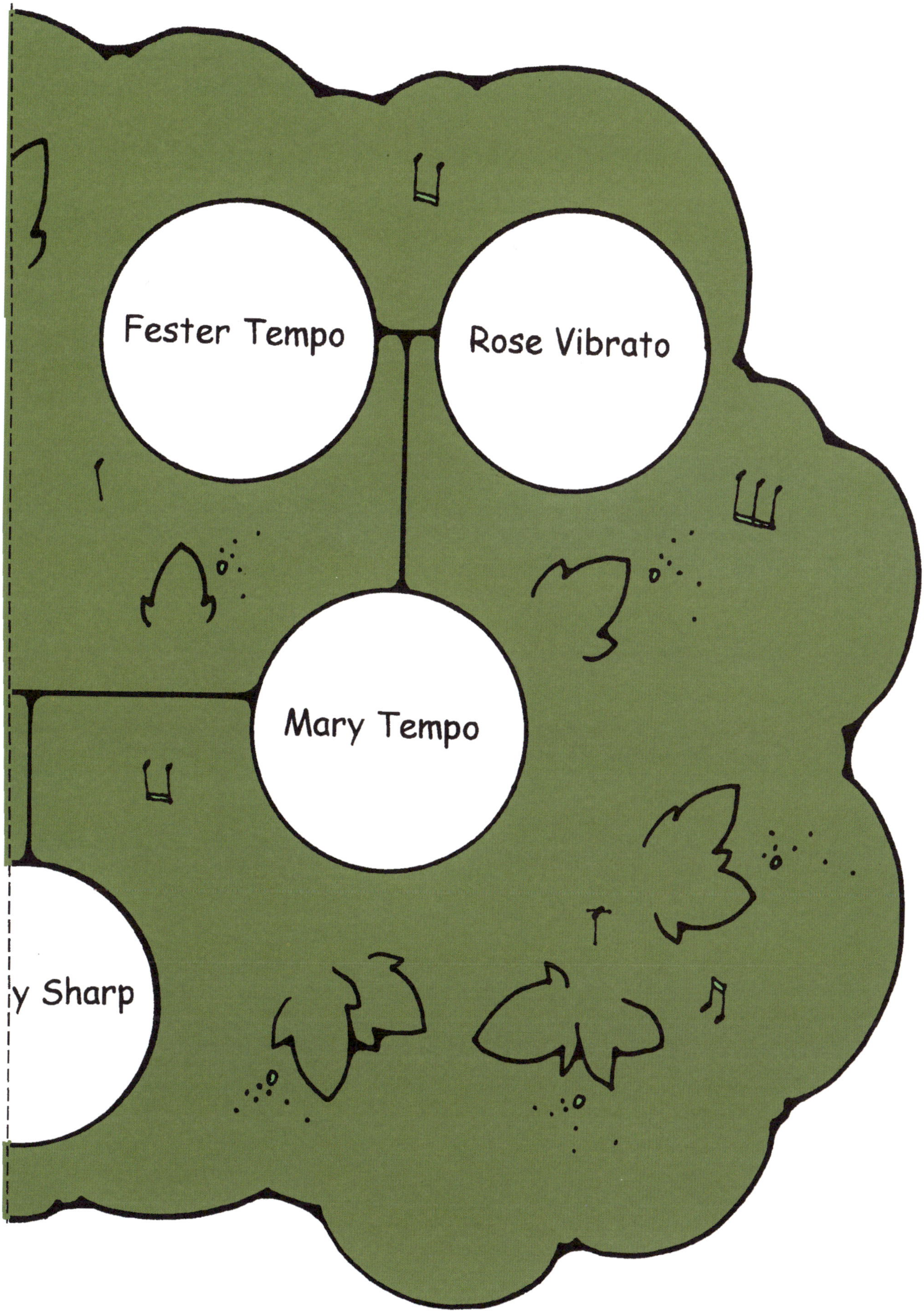

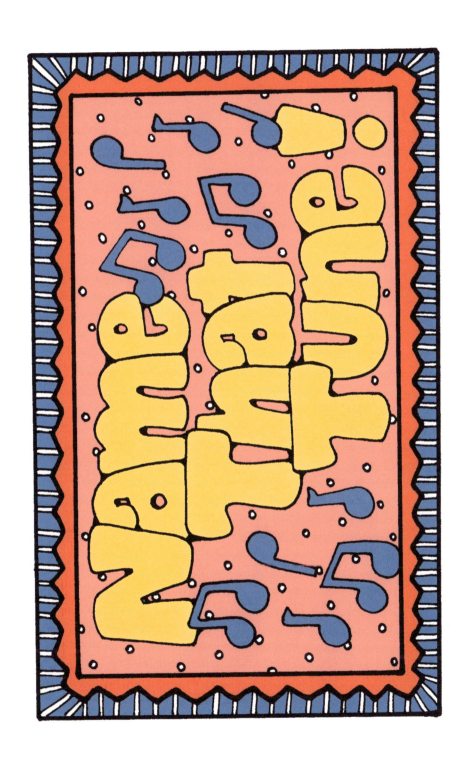

NAME THAT TUNE SONGS from the *Children's Songbook*:

- I Am a Child of God 2
- I Lived in Heaven 4
- I Know My Father Lives 5
- I Thank Thee, Dear Father .. 7
- Can a Little Child like Me ... 9
- A Child's Prayer 12
- Children All Over the World 16
- Thanks to Our Father 20
- We Bow Our Heads 25
- Reverently, Quietly 26
- This Is God's House 30
- He Sent His Son 34
- Away in a Manger 42
- Jesus Once Was a Little Child 55
- Tell Me the Stories of Jesus 57
- Jesus Wants Me for a Sunbeam 60
- Jesus Said Love Everyone .. 61
- I Feel My Savior's Love 74
- The Church of Jesus Christ 77
- I'm Trying to Be Like Jesus 78
- When He Comes Again 82
- The Golden Plates 86

- I Love to See the Temple .. 95
- Faith 96
- Baptism 100
- The Still Small Voice 106
- Seek the Lord Early 108
- Search, Ponder, and Pray .. 109
- Follow the Prophet 110
- Book of Mormon Stories .. 118
- Nephi's Courage 120
- Latter-day Prophets 134
- Love One Another 136
- Where Love Is 138
- I'll Walk with You 140
- Keep the Commandments .. 146
- Dare to Do Right 158
- Choose the Right Way 160
- I Will Be Valiant 162
- I Am like a Star 163
- I Will Follow God's Plan ... 164
- I Want to Be a Missionary Now 168
- I Hope They Call Me on a Mission 169
- We'll Bring the World His Truth 172
- Teach Me to Walk in the Light 177

- Families Can Be Together Forever 188
- Love Is Spoken Here 190
- Saturday 196
- When We're Helping 198
- When Grandpa Comes 201
- Pioneer Children Sang As They Walked 214
- I Often Go Walking 202
- Mother Dear 206
- Mother, I Love You 207
- Daddy's Homecoming 210
- My Heavenly Father Loves Me 228
- "Give," Said the Little Stream 236
- In the Leafy Treetops 240
- Popcorn Popping 242
- Once There Was a Snowman 249
- Fun to Do 253
- I Have Two Little Hands .. 272
- Head, Shoulders, Knees, and Toes 275
- Do As I'm Doing 276
- Hinges 277
- Wise Man and the Foolish Man 281
- Happy, Happy Birthday ... 284

Activity #13: Pick-a-card

Use this to help children sing songs in a variety of ways and keep them interested in the songs.

TO MAKE:
Mount cards (pages 103-110) on cardstock paper and cut out. Laminate for durability.

TO USE:
1. Pick a card in one of the following ways: Pick cards out of a bag or container, spread cards out in your hand like a deck of cards, or lay cards face down and choose one at a time.
2. Sing the songs chosen according to what the card shows, as follows: if the "Teachers choice" card is drawn, leader chooses a teacher to tell how the song should be sung, e.g., faster, slower, softer, louder, or hum. If the "A capella" card is chosen, sing without the piano. If the "Girls only" card is chosen, then only the girls sing. If the "Wearing white" card is chosen, have all children who are wearing white sing, etc.

Activity #14: Singing Simon

This activity motivates children to sing the ways you ask them, e.g., louder, softer, slower, faster

TO MAKE:
1. Mount the snake pieces (pages 111-116) on cardstock paper, laminate, and cut out.
2. Cut a slit on the dashed lines on parts A and C and insert part B (center piece) to slide snake back back and forth.

TO USE:
1. Show children how Simon the snake can expand to grow longer or push together to become shorter.
2. Tell children that Simon the snake is watching with his big eyes to see if they are singing well.
3. As children sing the songs, Simon shows how they sing. Have someone be the judge and pull the snake out (to expand) if they sing well, or push the snake in if they don't sing well or as directed.
4. Reward children for singing well with "You're ssssinging is sssuper!" badge or medallion. (See Super Singer Awards in the back of this book.)

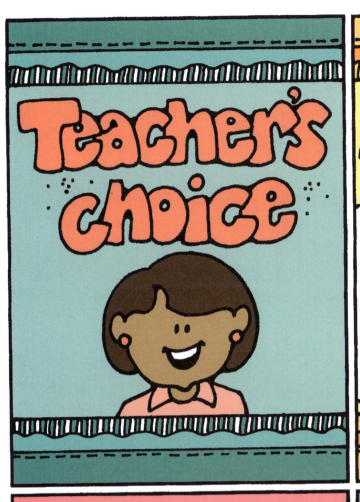
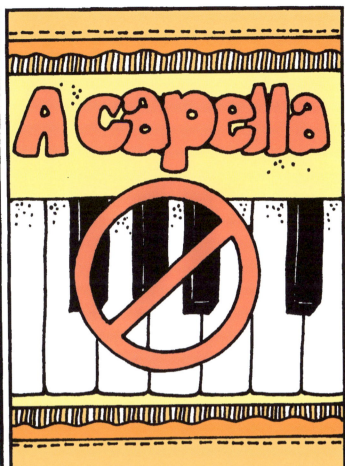

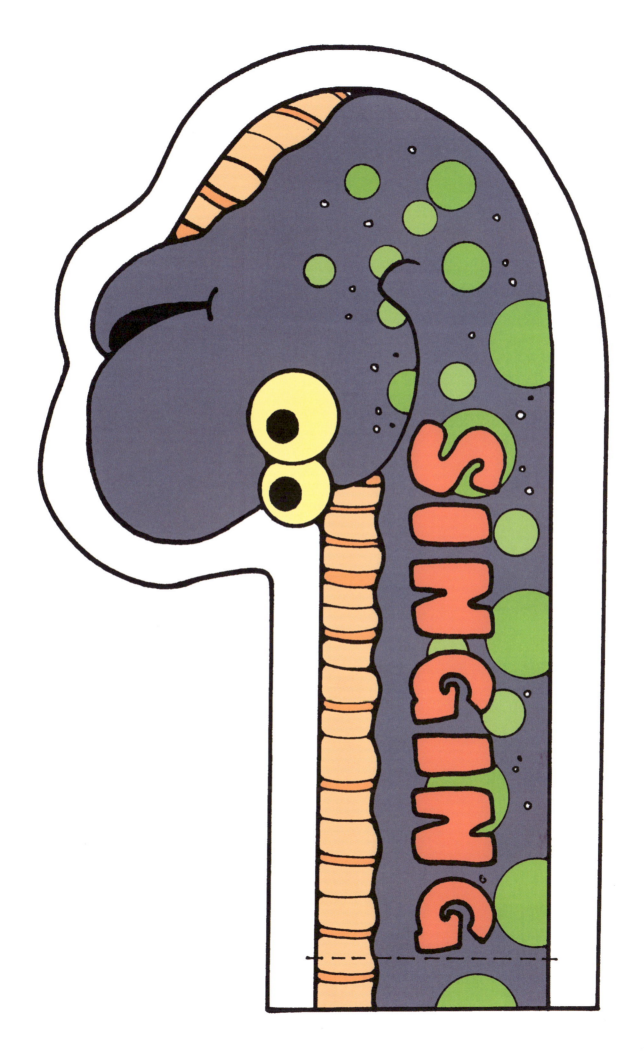

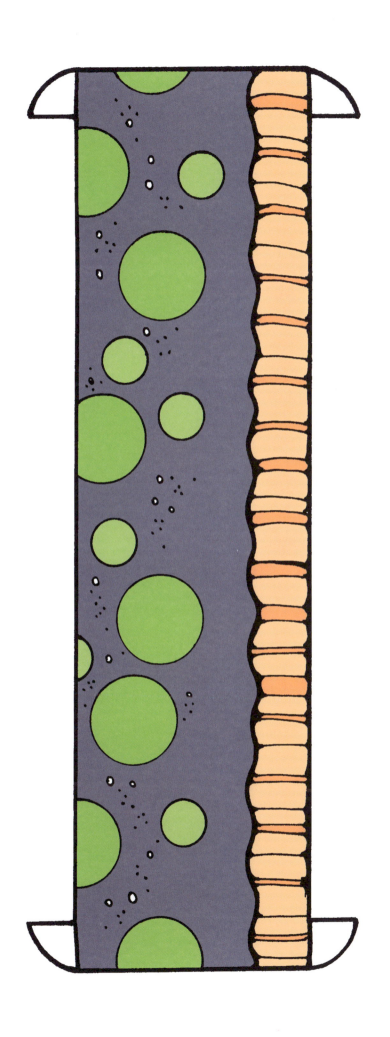

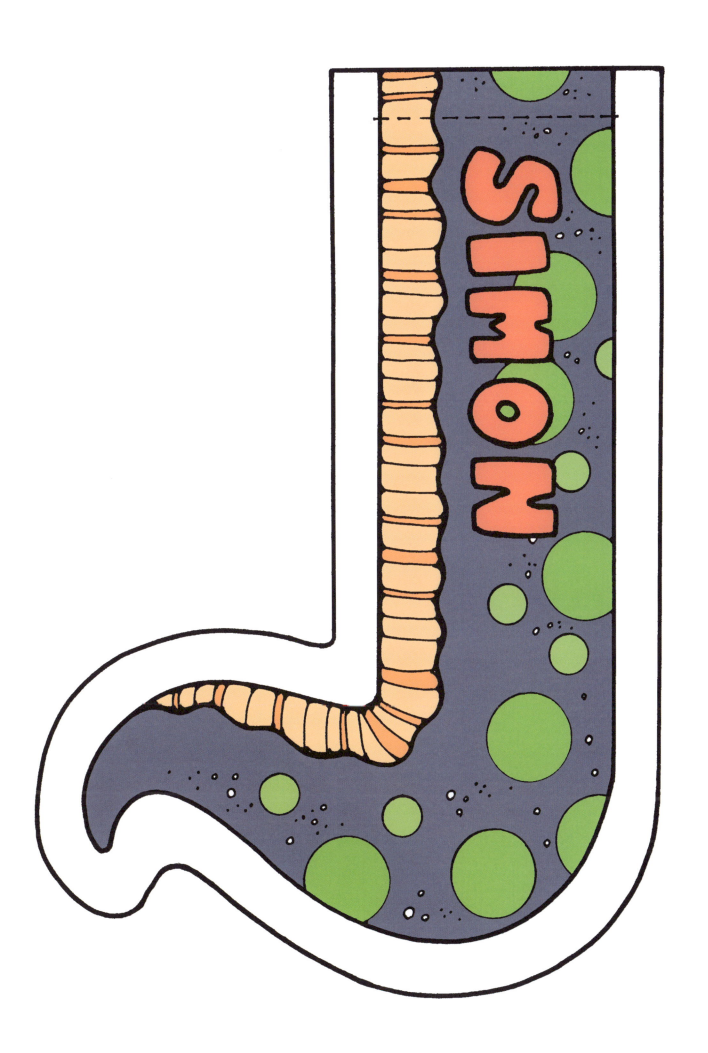

Activity #15: Stop and Go!

Use this attention getter to keep children on their toes. Warn them that if they are not paying attention they may be singing alone!

TO MAKE:
Mount the signs (pages 119-122) on cardstock paper, cut out, and laminate. *Optional:* Attach a popsicle stick or tongue depressor on the back of the sign for easy holding.

TO USE:
When you or a child hold up the GO sign, everyone is to sing. When you or the child hold up the STOP sign, everyone is to be silent.

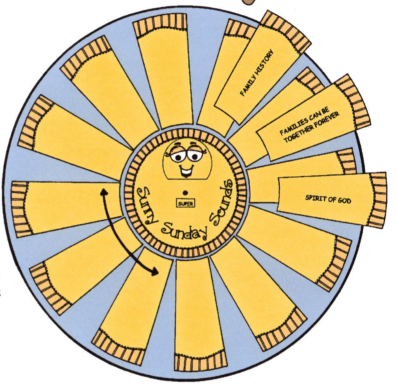

Activity #16: Sunny Sunday Sounds

Use the visuals as a singing gauge or a singing chart. The singing gauge determines how well they sing. The singing chart helps you to determine which songs you sing (using the sun rays).

TO MAKE:
1. To create the face poster, cut out and mount the faces wheel (page 123) on the center of a large poster. Laminate the poster.
2. To create the *Sunny Sunday Sounds* wheel, cut out and mount the wheel (page 125) on cardstock paper. Cut out the rectangle (where the words peer through) and circle (where the faces peer through) where indicated on the wheel. Laminate the wheel.
3. Attach the Sunny Sunday Sounds wheel to the poster over the faces wheel using a paper fastener or metal brad.
4. To create the sun rays (pages 127-134), mount rays on cardstock paper, laminate, and cut out. Draw a large circle on the poster to frame sun rays (see method below*). Write the titles and page numbers of the songs you wish children to sing on slips of paper and tape one to each sun ray (as shown above). These could be songs you are practicing during the year for the Primary program.

*How to Draw Circle: Tie a pencil or marker to one end of an 8" string and hold the other end of the string in the center of the wheel. Holding the string tight, place the pencil on the poster starting on the left or right side and draw the circle line.

TO USE:
Option #1: Have a child or leader turn the wheel to the face and word that describes how they are singing, e.g.: super, good, so-so, or poor.
Option #2: As children learn songs, place the sun rays on the chart, or post them all on the chart and take them off as they learn the songs.

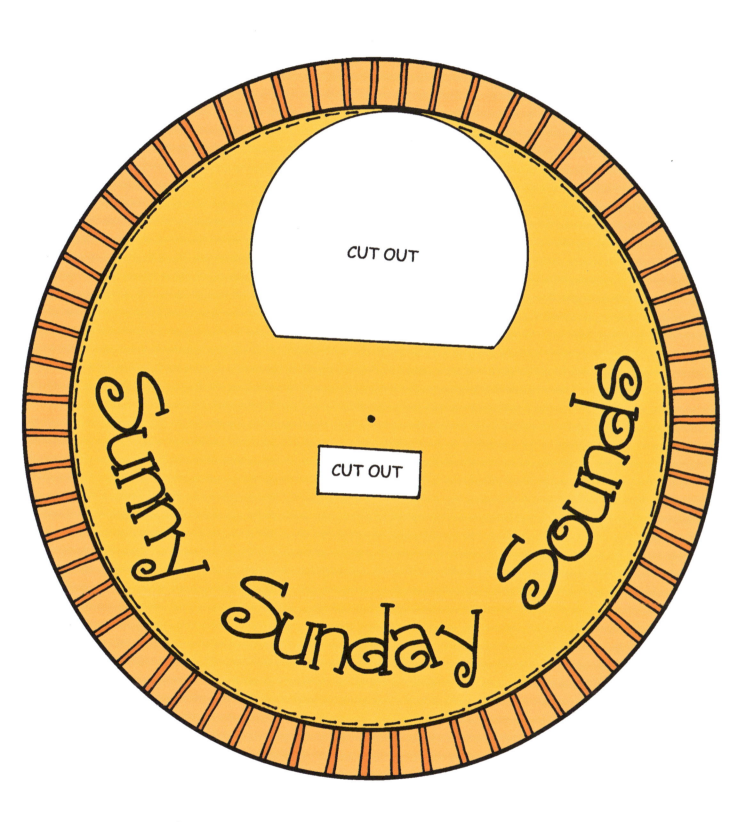

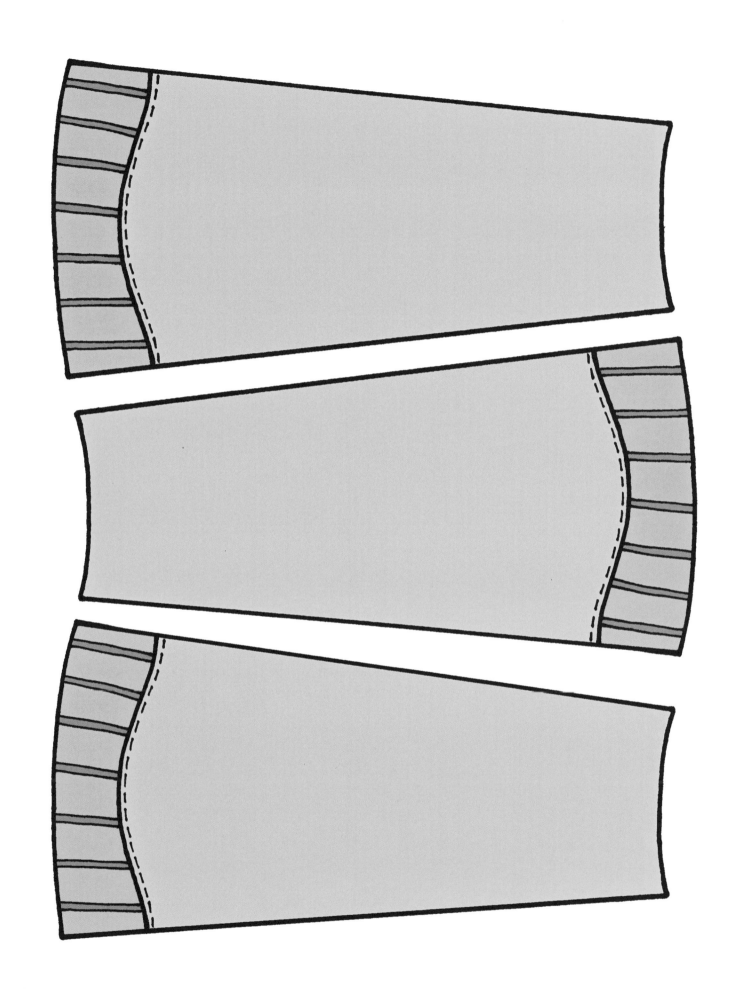

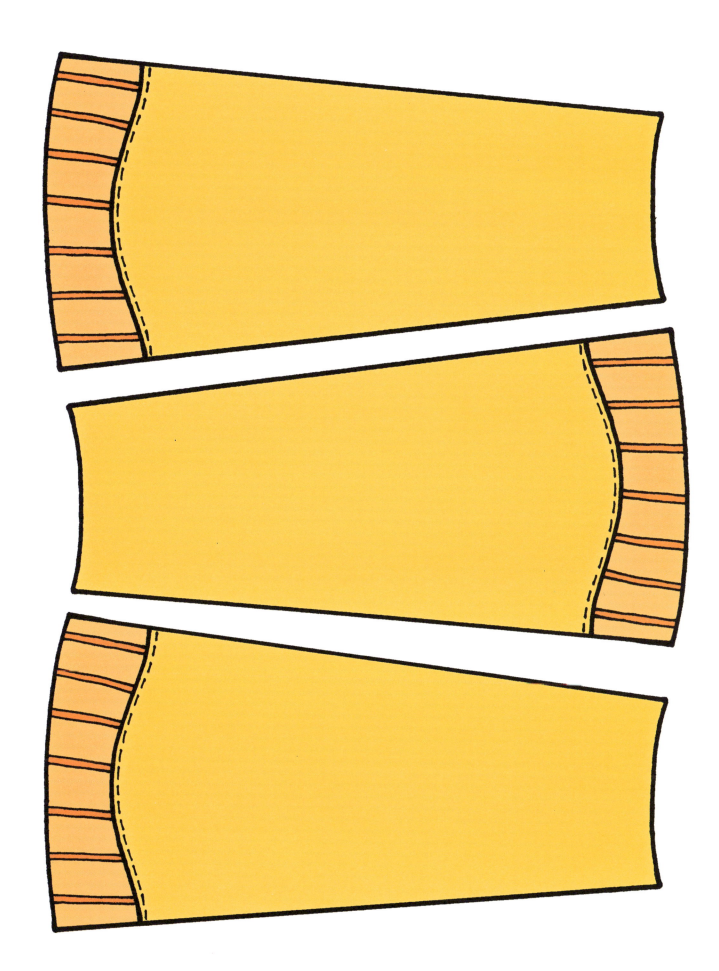

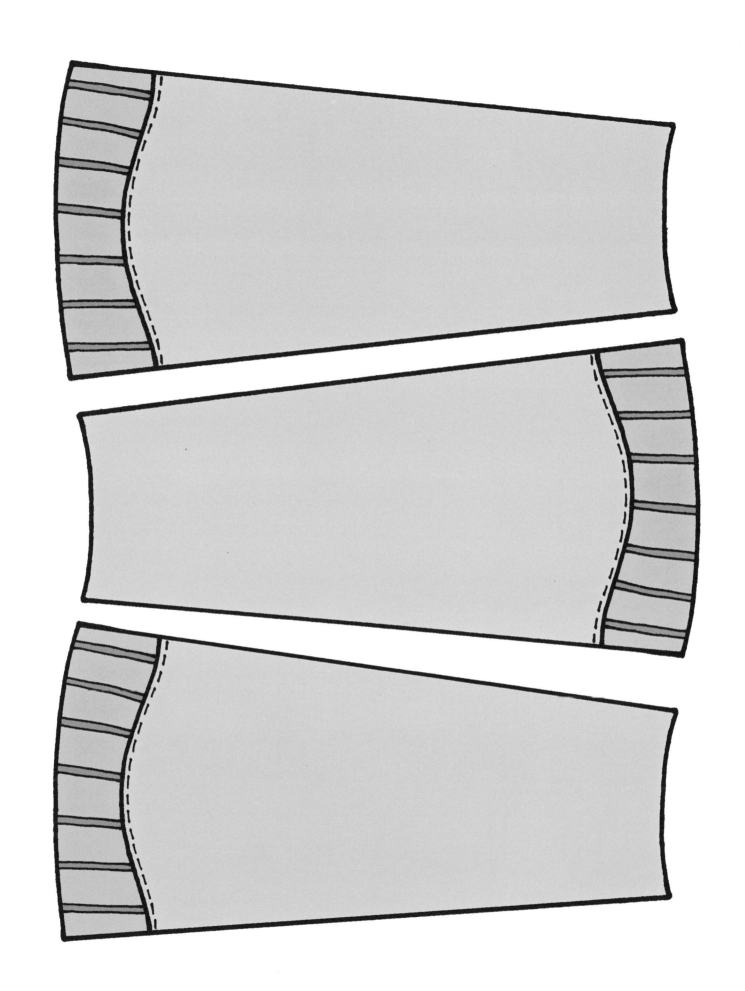

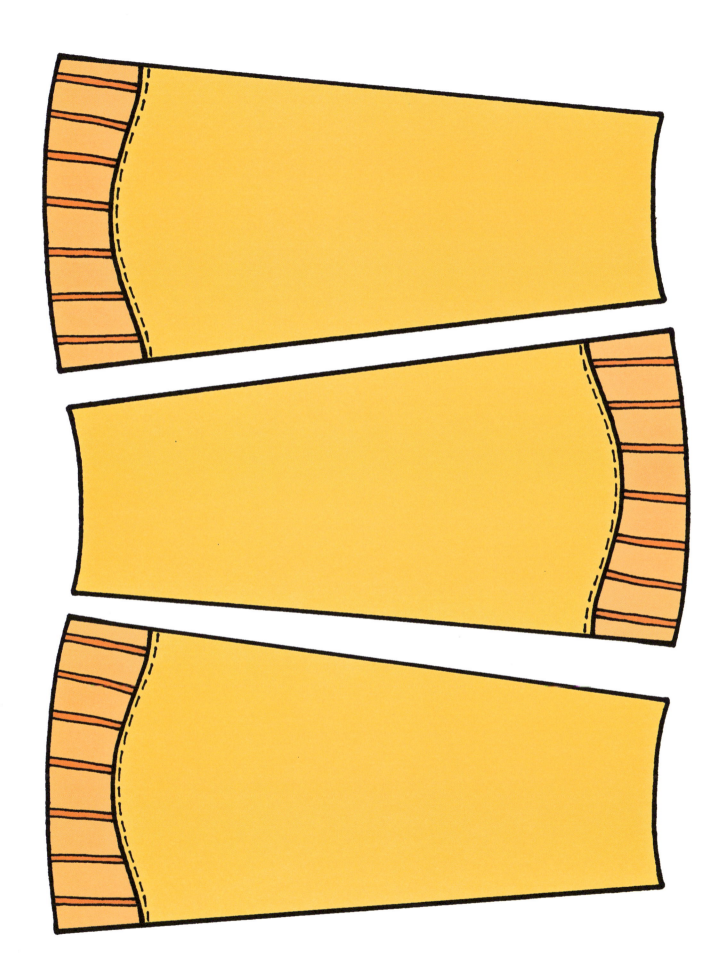

Super Singing Activities

Sing standing up.
Sing with arms folded.
Sing with eyes closed.
Sing turned around.
Boys only sing.
Girls only sing.
Sing with head hanging down.
Sing standing on your left leg only.
Sing holding your nose.
Sing facing the person next to you.
Sing holding your hands behind your back.
Sing looking up.

Activity #17: Temple Flowers: "Bee" a Singer

Children can choose a flower to select a song and a bee to select a the way to sing a song, e.g., with eyes closed.

TO MAKE:
1. Cut out and mount the temple, and temple grounds (pages 137-141) on a large poster and laminate the entire poster.
2. Cut out the flowers and bees (pages 143-145) and mount on cardstock paper, and laminate.
3. Write the names and page numbers of the songs children are familiar with on the backs of the 12 flowers.
4. On the back of each of the 6 bees, write an action (examples shown left).
5. Tape the bees on the temple grounds, and tape the flowers over the bees to hide them behind each flower.

TO USE:
Ask children to come up and choose a flower. Sing the song on the back of the flower chosen. If a child finds a bee behind the flower, ask children to sing the song the way the bee suggests (see #4 above).

All images can be printed in color or black and white, using the Super Singing Activities CD-ROM.

Do not cut on the dotted line. Use this margin to mount the other side.

Do not cut on the dotted line. Use this margin to mount the other side.

Activity #18: Super Singer Awards

Use these super singer awards to motivate children to be super singers. Give to children as badges or medallions. If you need to make additional awards, these can be printed from the CD-ROM.*

TO MAKE:
Cut out and laminate (if desired) to give out as children show they are "super singers" by participating, listening, sitting reverently, and learning the words.

TO USE:
1. Attach award to child's clothing with a safety pin or tape.
2. Attach a string so the child can wear it around his or her neck, or on wrists as a wristband.
3. Sometimes you can attach (tape or staple) treats such as taffy or Smarties (tart candies).

Note: When giving the angel award, explain that angels don't have wings. Wings are a symbol that angels can go from heaven to earth.

*All images can be printed in color or black and white, using the *Super Singing Activities* CD-ROM.

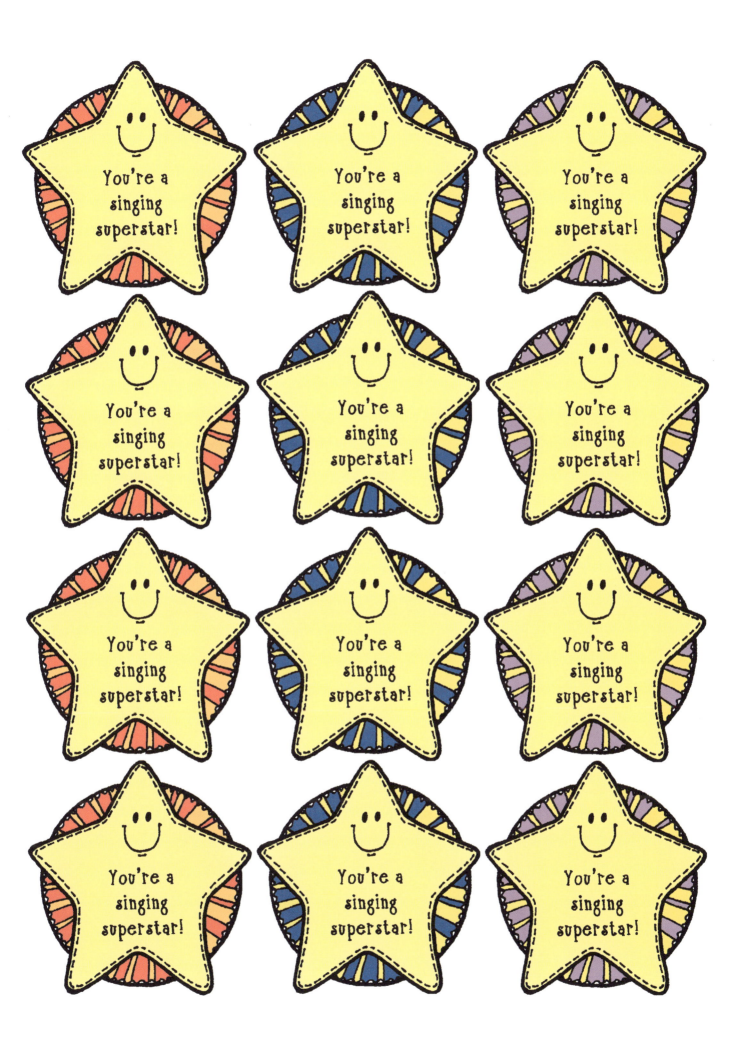

Enjoy More Full-Color, Ready-to-Use Books and CD-ROMS:

With these colored, ready-to-use visuals, you can create memorable learning activities and motivate children to sing and learn in family home evening and Primary. They are also available on CD-ROM so you can print images in color or black-and-white.

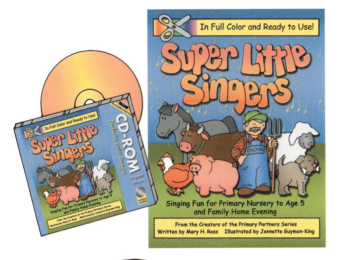

Super Little Singers

You'll find: singing motivators, visuals, and action activities for 28 songs (21 from the *Children's Songbook*). Enjoy using the visuals for these seven all-time favorite children's songs: Ants Go Marching, Eensy Weensy Spider, Five Little Ducks, Five Little Speckled Frogs, Old MacDonald, Twinkle, Twinkle, Little Star, and Wheels on the Bus.

Enjoy More Full-color, Ready-to-use Activities

Preview of
Gospel Fun Activities

Quick-and-Easy Family Home Evenings and Sharing Time

In minutes you can teach a child basic principles of the gospel from the post-and-present games and activities in this book. As a picture is worth 1,000 words, we have created the visuals that will help you teach the gospel with very little effort. These teaching tools are easy to present by mounting them on a poster, board, or wall. Children enjoy creating and presenting the activities, so put them in charge whenever you can.

These *Gospel Fun Activities* are ideal for family home evening and Primary sharing time. Parents can use the activities and thought treats to simplify family home evening lessons and make learning fun. Primary leaders and teachers can use the ideas to create sharing time presentations and add to lessons.

The visuals are ready-to-use to post and present, helping you teach the following Gospel subjects: Accountability, Choose the Right, Commandments, Faith, Follow Jesus, The Holy Ghost, Missionary Talents, Missionary Work, Repentance, Second Coming, Service, and Testimony.

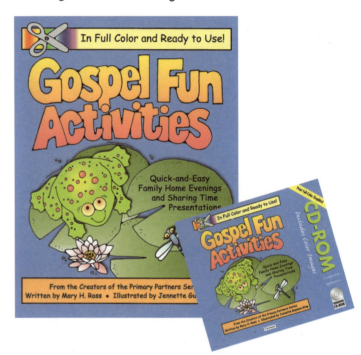